The Blessing Of Serving Another Man's Ministry

Seven Serving Secrets That Will Sentence You To Success!

Greg Mauro

Greg Mauro Ministries

Copyright © 2012 by Greg Mauro

All rights reserved.

No portion of this book may be reproduced in any form without written permission from the publisher or author, except as permitted by U.S. copyright law.

Scripture Acknowledgements

All Scripture quotations, unless otherwise indicated, are taken from the *King James Version* of the Bible, Public Domain.

Scripture quotations marked **NKJV** are from the *New King James Version®. Copyright © 1982 by Thomas Nelson. Used by permission. All rights reserved.*

Scripture quotations marked **NLT** are from the *Holy Bible, New Living Translation, copyright © 1996, 2004, 2015 by Tyndale House Foundation. Used by permission of Tyndale House Publishers, Inc., Carol Stream, Illinois 60188. All rights reserved.*

Scripture quotations marked **NIV** are from the *Holy Bible, New International Version®, NIV®. Copyright © 1973, 1978, 1984, 2011 by Biblica, Inc.™ Used by permission. All rights reserved worldwide.*

What Leaders Say About Greg Mauro

"I have witnessed firsthand the great blessing Greg has been to Dr. Cerullo's life and ministry, and have seen his own life and ministry flourish as he has served and received the impartation of his mentor. These nuggets from Greg's years of experience will take your Christian experience to another level."
— **Pastor Tommy Barnett**, Senior Pastor, Phoenix First Assembly and Founder, Los Angeles Dream Center

"This immensely thought-provoking work is one that is well overdue and addresses a vital subject that few have attempted to resolve. The wisdom in this book breaks new ground and will possibly become a classic in this and the next generation. Every sentence of this book is pregnant with revelation. I admonish every leader to plunge into this ocean of knowledge and practical wisdom and activate the blessing of serving another man's vision."
— **(The Late) Dr. Myles Munroe**, Bahamas Faith Ministries International

"In a time when those called to ministry desire to lead others, Greg reveals the key of ministry is learning to serve others. Greg has been faithful to Dr. Cerullo for decades as Elisha to Elijah. Discover what he has learned and apply these principles that will 'sentence you to success'!"
— **Perry Stone**, Voice of Evangelism

"Greg Mauro has been the right-hand man to Evangelist Morris Cerullo for many years. Each time I have met with him I have been impressed by his very efficient servanthood and his sincere desire to make life easier for Brother Cerullo. The secrets to tapping into the blessing he has written about in this book are tried and tested through his years of serving. God bless you, Greg, for writing such a book!"
— **Dr. Stephan K. Munsey, Ph.D.**, Sr. Pastor, Family Christian Center, Munster, Indiana

"As the Hispanic voice for Dr. Morris Cerullo for many years, I have not ever known a man, anointed and called by God, that has served with such passion, intensification, and loyalty, as Greg Mauro. Greg has written in this book such powerful secrets of deep revelation regarding the calling to serve others, that anyone who reads this book will never again refuse to serve another man's ministry."
— **Dr. Hernan Castano, Senior Pastor Iglesia Rio De Acete**

"It is my honor and privilege to recommend The Blessing of Serving Another Man's Ministry. *I am convinced that the Christian Church has inadvertently taught that unless someone is the main man, they are of no value. For decades, Greg has walked behind Dr. Cerullo, sharing the burden of ministry and freeing him to follow God's voice and vision."*
— **Dr. Stephen L. Lowery**, Former President, National Church of God

"Greg Mauro has spent the majority of his life defining what it means to have integrity, faithfulness, and commitment. This book will show the importance of a servant's heart, and how even though one's work may go unseen, their role is important and their impact is great. For anyone who needs a reminder of the joys and rewards of living a faithful life, I would highly recommend this work."
— **Pastor Matthew Barnett**, Co-founder of the Dream Center

Contents

Prologue: A Life Forever Changed	VIII
	XI
Foreword (Written by Dr. Morris Cerullo in 2014)	XIII
1. When Your Yes Becomes His More!	1
2. The Secret Of Honor	11
3. The Secret of Obedience	16
4. The Secret of Flexibility	22
5. The Secret of Faithfulness	30
6. The Secret Of Being Proactive	39
7. Receiving the Mantle of Your Mentor	48
8. About The Author	57
9. Photo Gallery	59

Prologue: A Life Forever Changed

First, thank you for picking up this third edition of *The Blessing of Serving Another Man's Ministry*.

The first edition was written in 2012—on the 25th anniversary of my ministry of serving by the side of Dr. Morris Cerullo—at his encouragement. Now, five years after he has been promoted to heaven, I find myself writing with fresh perspective.

People often ask me, "Are you doing anything different now that Dr. Cerullo is in heaven?" My answer is simple: I'm doing exactly what I did when he was alive—extending his ministry, his voice, and his dream. What you're about to read next is exactly what I wrote the morning I woke up on July 10, 2020, to the news that my friend, mentor, and spiritual father had been promoted to glory:

"For 33 years, I had the privilege of knowing and serving the most remarkable man I have ever met.

On **July 10, 2020**, at approximately 8:45 PM—clutching his beloved Bible—Morris Cerullo breathed his last breath on earth and his first in heaven, welcomed by a great cloud of witnesses and greeted by the words we all long to hear:

"Well done, good and faithful servant!"
(Matthew 25:23)

Morris Cerullo will go down as one of God's greatest pioneers and spiritual generals of all time.

I was privileged to call him a friend, a father, a mentor, a prophet, an example, a prayer partner, a corrector, an encourager—and so much more.

He taught me to believe that with God, **all things are possible** *(Mark 9:23)* —for me.

He took a tall, insecure accounting graduate straight from college and made me a crusade director, vice president, promoter, media buyer, author, preacher, television host, worship leader, emcee, event planner, husband, and father... and most of all, his son.

He taught me so many things:

- "Inspect what you expect."

- "To accept excuses is to accept failure."

- "The key to success is dealing with people, places, and things as they are, not as you wish they were."

- "God isn't depending on anything we possess—He's depending on what we'll let Him make of us."

- "The key to breakthrough is timing."

- "All truth is parallel."

And above all, he taught me to love God more... and to love people more.

Some people talk about leaving a legacy. Morris Cerullo **built** a Legacy Center.

He has trained and impacted millions of spiritual leaders across the globe—including me. **We are his legacy.**

His life's cry was that God would give him the ability to **pass on the anointing, the grace, and the power** from his life to ours. That cry did not die with him.

While Morris now cheers us on from the grandstands of heaven, the Bible teaches us that **no anointing ever leaves the earth—it either lies dormant -- or when picked up it intensifies** *(2 Kings 2:9–15)*.

Morris also taught us this truth: **This ministry will never die, because it is not the work of a man—but the work of the Holy Spirit.**

I am a recipient of this and so much more. By the grace of God, may my life carry the legacy of the man, the ministry, and the message of my friend and spiritual father, Morris Cerullo."

Now, as I approach my 40th year of serving the ministry of Dr. Cerullo, I am more convinced than ever that the lessons I learned serving are timeless. They have shaped not only my ministry, but my life. In the pages that follow, I will share the seven most important things I learned—and continue to learn—about the blessing of serving another man's ministry. It is my prayer that these truths will inspire, challenge, and equip you to step into God's greater purpose for your life, just as they have for mine.

Dedication

When I first sat down to write this book in 2012, my desire was simple: to share the seven greatest lessons I have learned from serving the ministry of Dr. Morris Cerullo—truths that have profoundly blessed and shaped my own life. Like the Apostle Paul, I did not want to "speak of anything except what Christ has accomplished through me" (Romans 15:18). I wanted this book to be practical, authentic, and from the heart—speaking to those who know they are called to serve another person's ministry, and to those who might be surprised to discover that calling along the way.

I wrote it simply in obedience to the Lord and at the encouragement of Dr. Morris Cerullo as we celebrated our 25th year of serving together. I could never have imagined how far God would allow it to go. I am deeply grateful for every pastor, leader, and reader who has picked up a copy, shared it with others, or offered a kind word of encouragement. Your support has blessed my life more than you know and has helped this message of serving another man's ministry reach far beyond anything I could have accomplished alone. Thank you.

This edition is lovingly dedicated to the legacy of my spiritual father, mentor, and friend, Dr. Morris Cerullo, who went home to be with the Lord on July 10, 2020, and to his precious wife, my spiritual mother, Theresa Cerullo, who joined him in heaven two years later. For more than seven decades, they faithfully carried the Gospel to the nations, impacting untold millions through Crusades, Schools of Ministry, and MCWE Conferences. That impact continues today as their powerful voice still reaches and trains countless lives through our Online Salvation Outreach and School of Ministry. You are the living proof that the vision God gave them is alive and thriving.

I also dedicate this book to my beautiful wife, Jeri—the love of my life, my partner in ministry, and my greatest encourager. Together, we have celebrated more than 25 years of marriage, and God has blessed us with a growing family that brings incredible joy: eight amazing children and thirteen beautiful grandchildren (and counting!). They truly are my greatest blessing for serving another man's ministry, and I am so proud of each one.

To the faithful staff of Morris Cerullo World Evangelism, who daily give their all to advance this vision, I dedicate this book with deep gratitude. To our President, David Cerullo, who carries the torch of this great work, I express my heartfelt thanks and honor.

Finally, I dedicate this book to the incredible partners and friends of MCWE. Your prayers and faithful support make it possible for us to continue fulfilling the Great Commission together. You are true heroes of the faith, and I honor you from the bottom of my heart.

Foreword (Written by Dr. Morris Cerullo in 2014)

It has been one of the great joys of our lives for Theresa and I to watch the anointing of God increase upon Greg's life these past twenty-five years.

Greg has become more than a blessing—he is a dear spiritual son and an extension of my ministry. His life has literally demonstrated the message in the pages of *"The Blessing of Serving Another Man's Ministry."* He has flourished as he has served and received the impartation from my life and ministry to his.

Those that come under the special anointing imparted in this book truly become an extension of what it really means to be a disciple of Christ.

God called Greg as an accounting student from Oral Roberts University with a passion to reach the world for Jesus, to come and join the Morris Cerullo World Evangelism team in San Diego in 1987.

As he showed himself faithful over time, I will never forget then sending him to live in England with his young family and serve as my European Director for almost seven years.

Together we saw Great Britain shaken as 16,000 plus a night jammed the historic Earl's Court Auditorium for annual week-long Mission to London meetings, 50,000 pack the Olympic Stadium over three nights in Moscow, Russia, just months after the Iron Curtain came down, pioneer Christian television across Europe and so much more...

Over the years, Greg has served as my crusade director, television co-host, writer, accountant, media buyer, marketing and public relations man, emcee of my conferences, and most of all my associate minister.

Every pastor, leader, believer that wants God to use their life in a greater way will be deeply blessed and enriched by the encouraging words of this book.

I highly recommend every pastor and spiritual leader who truly wants an armor bearer to seed this message into their lives. You will be rewarded with a ministry of faithfulness.

God's servant,

Morris Cerullo

Morris Cerullo

CHAPTER ONE

When Your Yes Becomes His More!

*"**G**reg, what would you think if I called you to serve another man's ministry that had the same vision that I have put in your heart, and by doing so, you would reach more people for My Kingdom than if you did so on your own?"*

A Life-Changing Encounter on the ORU Bridge

The place I will forever remember it as though we were standing there now as you read these words—the walking bridge connecting the student parking lot to the bustling campus of Oral Roberts University, where the grand buildings and space-age architecture were a daily reminder to the thousands of us students of Dr. Oral Roberts' charge to "Make no small plans here."

The Time: April 1987

With a mere six weeks remaining before graduation, and with a dream in my heart far bigger than myself, I was ready to go from this incredible place of preparation to be used by God to fulfill the Great Commission and reach our world for Christ.

Having no idea that I was about to have a life-changing encounter that would set the course for my spiritual future in ways I would never have imagined when I woke up almost late for class that beautiful spring morning in Tulsa.

Serving as a youth pastor in a local church, as a worship leader in another, carrying a ten-foot cross and sharing the Gospel with whomever would listen across Tulsa, preaching on the streets outside bars, leading evangelistic teams to Florida's beaches during spring break to witness to the masses of college students—now coupled with my ORU experience, I was ready to spread my wings and take the next exciting step in God's unfolding plan.

I drove my old car from the student apartments to campus, parked in the lot outside the Mabee Center, and began my trek to class.

I had done it hundreds of times. Grab my books, slam the car door, and begin my brisk walk with a spring in my step to be sure I got to the first class of the day on time.

Connecting the parking lot and the campus is a simple white cement walking bridge spanning across a creek that divides the lot from the ORU campus—a well-traveled daily route. But I was soon to find out that this day would be unlike any other.

As I set foot on the bridge, I encountered a tangible presence and heard a voice that I knew all too well—that stopped me in my tracks. Students scurrying to class by the scores walked past me as I stood still at the midpoint of this small bridge. Perhaps a minute passed, and now I was standing alone on the bridge, unexpectedly stopped by a wonderful presence and challenged by the unmistakable voice of the Holy Spirit.

The words are as fresh today as they were in 1987:

"Greg, what would you think if I called you to serve another man's ministry that had the same vision that I have put in your heart, and by doing so, you would reach more people for My Kingdom than if you did so on your own?"

I stood motionless, pondering this heavenly proposition.

A few straggling students passed by on the bridge, I'm sure wondering if this skinny six-foot-nine motionless statue of a fellow student had lost his marbles!

Knowing how I responded to this divine moment would surely set the course for God's future plans for my life. And marveling at what a gentleman our God is—to present a "What would you think?" question, and not some "Thus saith the Lord, you will do such and such" command!

I stood there and pondered:

- Give up the idea of launching "my own" ministry?

- Serve someone else's ministry that had the same heart as I do?

- Reach more people?

- Be more effective for the Kingdom of God?

The more I mulled it over, it was a clear no-brainer!

"Sure, Lord. If I can be more fruitful and reach more for You by helping someone else that is already doing what You have put in my heart to do, then count me in!"

Another Life-Changing Encounter

Two weeks later, the ORU chapel service guest minister was introduced to the students—worldwide evangelist, apostle, and prophet Dr. Morris Cerullo. Another life-changing encounter.

As this servant of God spoke from the words of John 6:28, *"What must we do that we might work the works of God?"*, the Mabee Center chapel shook as the anointing of the Holy Spirit was poured out mightily upon the students.

Soon all were out of their seats, dropped to their knees, and crying out for God to use their lives...

As was I.

As I slowly began to stand after this season of prayer and communion with God in this powerful chapel service, that same voice I encountered on the bridge spoke again:

"Greg, I am calling you to stand by Morris' side and help him in the ministry."

Immediately my plans to enroll in the ORU seminary that fall flashed before my mind's eye. I asked God, "What about my plans to attend seminary?" Now, many years later, God's four-word reply has proven over and over again to be the understatement of my life:

"This will be greater!"

The Blessings of Saying Yes

On my knees in that ORU chapel service, I could not have imagined the blessings that God had in store serving as the vice-president of Ministries for Dr. Morris Cerullo:

- Happily married to a beautiful, godly wife, Jeri that Morris and Theresa prayed into my life!

- Eight amazing children (seven sons and one beautiful daughter) that love the Lord. Each one received college scholarships. All the boys played college football – one played in the NFL for eight years, and today each one is making a great impact in their world.

- Thirteen adorable grandchildren and counting.

- A praying mother that loves and prays for me, our family, and the ministry of MCWE daily.

- A younger brother, Glenn, that has a heart of gold and another brother, Gary, who pastored one of the great churches in America.

The opportunity to stand by Dr. Cerullo's side as communism fell (as he prophesied for 14 consecutive years prior from the platform of the Royal Albert Hall) and conduct the first historic public crusade in Moscow before 50,000 in the Olympic Stadium in 1989.

To be a part of spiritual history in the UK as we pioneered week-long Mission to London outreaches from world-famous Earl's Court to capacity crowds of 16,000 per night for six successive years, that shook Britain and garnered unprecedented national and worldwide attention for the message of the power of the Gospel of Jesus Christ.

To preach by a spontaneous miracle to 200,000 protestors on the University Square in Bucharest, Romania following the fall of the dictator Nicolae Ceausescu while I was there meeting with key leaders that had invited Dr. Cerullo to conduct a national School of Ministry and Crusade later that year. And so much more...

Now on my fourth passport, having been privileged to see millions saved, healed, set free, receive the impartation of the anointing, and being used by God on every continent—**yes, there is unquestionably an incredible blessing waiting for those that will rise up to accept the calling to serve another man's ministry.**

God Is Calling Those Willing to Rise Above the Culture Of Me!

In order to fully step into this blessing of serving we will have to rise above a culture and an era that celebrates the entrepreneur, the self-made man or woman that blazes his or her own trail. That same spirit has permeated the church, particularly the independent, Charismatic segments, where we are frequently bombarded with messages, encouragements, "words from the Lord," and marketing tools to launch your own ministry—get ordained, start your website, launch your own worldwide ministry and go!

In sharp contrast, Jesus said, *"And if ye have not been faithful in that which is another man's, who shall give you that which is your own?"* (Luke 16:12).

I think about the mother of James and John who came to Jesus with a heartfelt request—she wanted her sons to have a place of honor in His kingdom. It's easy to understand her desire; we all long to make our lives count. But Jesus responded by gently turning their idea of greatness upside down. He asked, *"Are you able to drink the cup that I am about to drink?"* (Matthew 20:22). And then He said something that still speaks to us today: *"Whoever desires to become great among you, let him be your servant"* (Matthew 20:26). He didn't condemn their longing to be used by God—but He redefined what true greatness looks like. In His kingdom, it's not about status or visibility, but about serving with His heart and following His example.

If we agree that there is a calling to serve another man's ministry, then it is my prayer that many who are reading this will rise up from their church pew as a spectator each Sunday and find an exciting, blessed place of service alongside the ministry they are a part of.

1 Corinthians 12:28 highlights the importance of the ministry of helps in the God-ordained structure of the church, listing it right after apostles, prophets, teachers, miracles, and gifts of healings:

"And God has appointed these in the church: first apostles, second prophets, third teachers, after that, miracles, then gifts of healings, ***helps,*** administrations, varieties of tongues."

The Ministry of Helps

Kim Harrington of MasterBuilder Ministries said it so well in her article on "The Ministry of Helps":

"People approach the church with pretty much the same consumer mentality they bring to the shopping mall—you better deliver the goods, be nice and user-friendly, or I'll simply take my business elsewhere. The concept of servanthood and faithfulness, sacrifice and dependability seems to be a thing of the past, or at least something that doesn't apply to church anymore.

The desperate need in all sorts of Christian ministries is for those who will dedicate themselves to the ministry of helps, a rather inglorious sounding title, but listed in order right after miracle and healing ministries in the above text. The Greek word translated 'helps' means 'to lay hold of, so as to support.' In other words, a minister of helps is someone who commits himself to another ministry in order to support and assist in any way he or she can.

I'm impressed by the ministry team of Billy Graham in this respect. One of the great reasons for his enormous success has to be the dedicated team that has worked with him since the early '50s—Cliff Barrows, George Beverly Shea, and others, have been with him from the very beginning. They didn't see their work with Billy as a stepping stone towards their own independent ministries, but rather as a lifetime calling.

And in the process of helping his ministry, they have achieved personal ministerial success that they never could have attained on their own. How many records has Bev Shea sold, how many millions of people has Barrows taught over the years, that never would have been possible outside of Billy Graham's ministry? When you commit yourself to the ministry of helps you lay hold of personal success that you might never have achieved otherwise."

Is there a Barnabas, a Silas, a Timothy, an Aquila/Priscilla reading this that is ready to serve the next Apostle Paul? Or a band of mighty men ready to serve the next David? An Elisha to serve the next Elijah? Or the next Kenneth Copeland that will serve the book table of the next Oral Roberts?

God has ordained an amazing journey for you, and Secret #1 to experiencing this incredible blessing is to say Lord, I am willing to serve as a number 2 or a number 3 or a number 4...

The Bible is filled with men and women who weren't in the spotlight, weren't "number one's" – weren't leading from the front—but their faith, obedience, and loyalty positioned them to impact the world in extraordinary ways." Just a few examples are:

- **Elisha** – the servant of Elijah who received a double portion and performed twice as many miracles.

- **Barnabas** – the encourager who believed in Saul when others feared him, and helped launch Paul's ministry.

- **Joshua** – Moses' assistant who led Israel into the Promised Land.

- **Timothy** – Paul's spiritual son who pastored one of the early church's most influential congregations.

- **Silas** – Paul's ministry companion who helped shake a prison with praise.

- **Aaron** – the spokesman for Moses, faithfully standing beside his brother.

- **Caleb** – not the leader of the spies, but the one who stood with Joshua in faith.

- **Jonathan** – heir to Saul's throne, yet laid it down for David, a man after God's heart.

- **Mordecai** – the humble guardian behind Queen Esther's rise and Israel's deliverance.

- **Andrew** – Peter's brother who quietly brought others to Jesus, including Peter himself.

- **Philip** – not one of the Twelve's inner circle, yet led a revival in Samaria and baptized the Ethiopian eunuch.

- **Naaman's servant girl** – unnamed and enslaved, yet she opened the door for his healing.

- **Joseph (husband of Mary)** – quietly protected and raised the Savior of the world.

- **Stephen** – not an apostle, but his martyrdom sparked the church's global expansion.

- **Apollos** – an eloquent teacher who helped establish the church in Corinth after Paul left.

Of those the Bible says were successful in everything they did, most found that success not by building their own ministry—but by faithfully serving someone else's, like Joseph, David, Joshua, Nehemiah and Abraham's servant, to name a few...

Joseph – Served Pharaoh

"The Lord was with Joseph, so ***he succeeded in everything he did***..." (Genesis 39:2 NLT) "The Lord was with him and caused everything he did to succeed." (Genesis 39:23 NLT)

David – Served Saul

"David continued to ***succeed in everything he did***, for the Lord was with him." (1 Samuel 18:14 NLT)

Joshua – Served Moses

"Be strong and very courageous and be careful to obey all the instructions Moses gave you...then ***you will be successful in everything you do***. Study this Book of instruction continually. Mediate on it day and night...only then will you prosper and succeed in all you do!" (Joshua 1:7-8 NLT)

As we turn the page together, I want to thank you for taking this journey with me...and to encourage you—this is where it gets personal. The next few chapters unpack some of the most important lessons I've learned on this journey. And if there's one thing I hope you'll discover, it's this: when you say yes to serving another person's dream, though it will cost you something, your yes never goes unnoticed in heaven. Your yes becomes Gods more!

Chapter Two

The Secret Of Honor

"Dear brothers and sisters, honor those who are your leaders in the Lord's work...show them great respect and wholehearted love because of their work." (1 Thess 5:12-13)

Honor Is More Than an Outward Display

I knew a man very well who went to work for a major ministry. He quickly worked his way into a position of leadership. Whenever he was in the presence of the president of the ministry, he was the picture of honor—serving water, juice, buckling him in the car, and displaying the most incredible outward show of respect you could imagine. But when he was not in the presence of his mentor, he would second-guess and make ever-increasing disparaging remarks.

This man had a hidden agenda. He was operating under the deception that he would one day take this man's ministry. Sadly, he eventually attempted to do so through a five-year series of frivolous and totally unsuccessful lawsuits against his mentor.

Today, this man is completely out of the ministry, while the man and the ministry he had hoped to highjack is thriving, reaching the world for Christ. **Honor is much more than an outward display or lip service.**

God Puts a High Premium on Honor

We serve a God who places a high premium on the character trait of honor. Yet we live in a day where there is an increasing lack of honor both inside and outside the church. Honor is simply defined as high respect toward someone or something.

It has been my honor to serve as the Vice-President of Ministries for Dr. Morris Cerullo for nearly four decades. How can we expect the blessing of God as we serve another person's ministry without heartfelt, abiding, and sincere honor and respect for our mentor?

Honor is referred to directly or indirectly over 400 times in Scripture as a command in both our horizontal relationships (with our spouse, employer, children, those in authority, etc.) and our vertical relationship with God the Father, Son, and Holy Spirit. Every dysfunction can be traced to a lack of honor for authority.

The first commandment with promise is: "**Honor your father and mother**, that your days may be long upon the land which the Lord your God is giving you." (Exodus 20:12)

1 Thessalonians 5:12-13 admonishes us, "We ask you, brothers and sisters, to acknowledge those who work hard among you, who care for you in the Lord and who admonish you. **Hold them in the highest regard in love because of their work.** Live in peace with each other."

1st Timothy 5:17 calls us to "Let the elders who rule well **be counted worthy of double honor**, especially those who labor in the word and doctrine.

Honor Releases God's Blessing

A great man once said, "All truth is parallel." Not only will we be blessed in the "land" God has given us when we honor our natural parents, but the same honor is a condition of God's blessing as it relates to our spiritual leaders. We live in a generation that openly celebrates dishonor and disrespect.

2 Timothy 3:1-2 foretold our day: *"This know also, that in the last days perilous times shall come. For men shall be lovers of their own selves, covetous, boasters, proud; blasphemers, disobedient to parents, unthankful, unholy..."*

Sadly, dishonor and second-guessing of our leaders runs rampant in the church today. Something as simple as referring to our pastor by his or her title—and not simply on a "buddy-buddy" first-name basis—shows respect. Too many today feel that first-name familiarity is appropriate under the misguided belief that there is no difference between the laity and the clergy.

The Sin of Over-Familiarity

Do you think over-familiarity with your spiritual leader or mentor can lead to disrespect? It did for Aaron and Miriam (Numbers 12:1-2). The Lord immediately called them to account:

"They (Aaron and Miriam) said, 'Has the Lord spoken only through Moses? Hasn't He spoken through us too?' But the Lord heard them... So immediately the Lord called out to Moses, Aaron, and Miriam and said, 'Go out to the tabernacle, all three of you!' And the Lord said to them, 'Now listen to what I have to say!'"

The Bible tells us that the Lord was very angry with them and struck Miriam with leprosy! (Numbers 12:9-10)

Some of the most "super-spiritual" believers are the ones who struggle the most with honoring their leaders. They feel that they have "arrived" and are on equal footing with anyone. While it is true that we are equal in relationship to God, we are different in function, and God expects that difference to be honored.

God expected it of the children of Israel, and He still expects it today.

Overfamiliarity is the enemy of honor. It tempts us to define others by what offends us rather than what God has placed inside them.

Overfamiliarity causes you to identify others by the least attractive, least prestigious aspect of their life. In Mark 6, Jesus fled the overfamiliarity and dishonor of His hometown. Power withdrew. Miracles ceased.

Dishonor says: "He's just..."

Honor says: "He's God's man."

Dishonor looks at weakness.

Honor sees divine purpose.

When we serve another man's ministry, this distinction becomes critical. Will we choose to value the one we serve as God sees them, or will we grow so used to their humanity that we miss their anointing?

Honor Brings Blessing to Your Life and Ministry

Honor is the currency of promotion. To serve another man's ministry in honor is to position yourself for promotion. Jesus said, "If anyone serves Me, him My Father will honor" (John 12:26).

Honor will take you where talent cannot.

Honor will open doors no man can shut.

Honor will keep you in position to receive all God wants to give through those He has called you to serve.

A return to biblical honor of our spiritual leaders is an indispensable key that will begin to release a new dimension of the blessing of God into your life, your family, and your ministry.

Secret #2: The Secret of Honor — *When you choose to honor the people God has placed in your life, you open the door for His blessing and favor.*

Your Call to Action

Honor is a choice. It begins in the heart and is expressed in both our words and actions. Take a moment and evaluate: Are you walking in true honor toward those God has placed in your life?

- Do you speak respectfully about your spiritual leaders when they are not around?

- Have you allowed over-familiarity to breed dishonor?

- Do you recognize and value the anointing on their life?

Ask God to show you any area where dishonor may have taken root. Repent, and choose to honor those He has placed over you. As you do, you will see the blessing and favor of God released in a greater measure.

"Outdo one another in showing honor" Romans 12:10

Chapter Three

The Secret of Obedience

Obedience Naturally Follows Honor

After the secret of honor, which we said is a sincere respect that comes from the heart, the character trait of obedience will naturally follow.

Obedience is coming under the authority of your mentor. In other words, submission. Elisha came under the authority of Elijah and received the blessing of the double portion:

"And so it was, when they had crossed over, that Elijah said to Elisha, 'Ask! What may I do for you, before I am taken away from you?' Elisha said, 'Please let a double portion of your spirit be upon me.' So he said, 'You have asked a hard thing. Nevertheless, if you see me when I am taken from you, it shall be so for you; but if not, it shall not be so.'" (2 Kings 2:9-10)

Elijah's charge to Elisha, *"If you see me when I am taken from you..."* speaks of Elisha staying connected to his mentor and paying close attention to his mentor.

A True Story: The Madrid Crusade

Here's a powerful true story that illustrates the blessing of obedience to your mentor.

For years, God had been stirring Dr. Cerullo's heart with a prophetic word: that a time was coming when He would use our ministry to shake the nation of Spain. That time finally came when I received an invitation from a precious pastor in Madrid, asking if Dr. Cerullo would consider coming to the Spanish capital.

Without delay, I got on a plane and met with a group of about twelve sincere and humble pastors from across Madrid. One pastored a church of 20 people, another 35, and the largest congregation had fewer than 200 members. Altogether, their combined attendance was maybe 600 people. Yet they were full of faith and vision, inviting Dr. Cerullo to conduct a crusade in a beautiful auditorium in the heart of Madrid that seated 1,200. For them, this would be the largest charismatic gathering they had ever seen. Their sincerity and purity of heart deeply moved me.

As was my custom, I called Brother Cerullo before leaving the city to give him a report. As I shared the news with excitement, he responded without hesitation:
"Greg, God showed me this crusade will be in a bull ring. Go back to the pastors and share what God is speaking to my heart."

When I returned to share his words, I watched their excitement shift to anxiety. You could see the concern in their eyes. A bull ring? That felt impossible. They asked if Dr. Cerullo would first come and hold the meeting in the auditorium and perhaps build toward a larger gathering in a bull ring the following year.

But I knew what the prophet of God had spoken. With as much grace and encouragement as I could offer, I reassured them that what God had revealed to Brother Cerullo would come to pass. I had seen it happen too many times before.

I extended my stay in Madrid, and with some hesitation, the pastors took me to look at several bull rings. Eventually, we settled on a brand-new one with a retractable roof, called *La Cubierta*—which in Spanish means "The Covering." It seated 12,000 people.

A Night We Will Never Forget

The day of the crusade finally arrived. That morning, the pastors gathered with me early for prayer and to help organize the setup. At 4 p.m., we held our ushers and workers meeting, and by 5 p.m., the doors to *La Cubierta* were opened. The pastors, now seated on the platform, bowed in prayer—hoping, believing, and waiting.

To their amazement, people began streaming in two full hours before the meeting was scheduled to begin. And the stream didn't stop. By 6 p.m., every seat in the 12,000-seat covered bull ring was filled. Even CNN was there, capturing the moment. The pastors' eyes were wide with awe, their faith soaring higher than ever. Yet none of us had any idea what was still to come.

As the powerful sound of Spanish praise and worship filled the arena, and the anointing of the Holy Spirit saturated the atmosphere, I stood to introduce Brother Cerullo. Holding his Bible high, he declared with authority:
"I greet you tonight in the Name that is above every name, Jesus Christ, the Son of the Living God!"

Moments later, as he preached under a mighty anointing, he boldly declared:
"Spain does not belong to the devil—Spain belongs to Jesus!"

As those prophetic words went forth, something extraordinary happened. Golf-ball-sized hail suddenly began pelting the platform and crowd—inside the covered bull ring! I looked up in disbelief. Sheets of white hail were falling from the sky... and the roof was closed.

The hail continued for several intense minutes. We rushed to cover Mrs. Cerullo with my jacket. Plastic tarps were thrown over the sound equipment and keyboard. Umbrellas popped up across the crowd. And yet, the prophet of God never flinched—he continued preaching as if the weather was perfect.

Finally, the hail subsided. I looked up again. The roof was still fully intact. There was no natural explanation. It was a supernatural sign and manifestation from Jehovah God!

Acknowledging what had just taken place, Dr. Cerullo lifted his voice and declared:

"The hail that fell in this arena is a sign of the blessing of God on the nation of Spain!"

The crowd erupted in spontaneous praise. That night, more than 10,000 souls came to Christ. Physical healings swept across the audience. Those pastors, their churches—and the nation of Spain—would never be the same again.

"Blessed rather are those who hear the word of God and obey it." Luke 11:28

The Secret of Obedience

What unfolded that unforgettable night in Spain was nothing short of miraculous—an undeniable demonstration of God's presence, power, and prophetic fulfillment. But none of it would have happened without a heart willing to obey—not just God's voice, but the spiritual authority He had placed in my life.

It all began with one of the most vital, yet often overlooked, secrets to unlocking the blessing of God over your life and ministry: obedience.

Secret #3: The Secret of Obedience — When you follow God's direction and honor the spiritual authority He has placed in your life, you don't just position yourself for favor and divine appointments—you become a servant to the greater vision God has entrusted to your leader. Obedience opens the door for something beyond your own plans—it allows you to participate in something God-sized.

How many times have we possibly stifled the work of God—not through rebellion, but simply through hesitation or a failure to support the vision He's given someone else? Sometimes your mentor may see what you cannot see—like Elijah saw what Elisha couldn't. But if you trust, if you obey, if you take the step even when it stretches you, you make room for God to do something greater through you than you could ever do alone.

This is the blessing of obedience. It's not just about following orders—it's about stepping into divine alignment with God's purpose, God's timing, and God's chosen vessels.

Your Call to Action!

1. **Examine your heart:** Are there areas where you've hesitated to obey God or the spiritual authority He has placed in your life? Take time to ask the Holy Spirit to reveal any resistance, and surrender those areas afresh to His leading.

2. **Reconnect with your leader's vision:** Ask yourself, *How can I better serve the vision God has given my pastor or mentor?* Look for one practical step you can take this week to support that vision with greater faith, humility, and initiative.

3. Choose alignment over ambition: In a world that celebrates self-promotion, ask God to help you value divine alignment more than personal advancement. Trust that obedience—even when you may not see the full picture—will always lead to something greater than you could have imagined.

Chapter Four

The Secret of Flexibility

Blessed Are The Flexible!

There may not be a greater secret to success in serving another **person's** ministry than being willing to be flexible.

Learning Flexibility From The Start

In the first chapter, I shared the unforgettable moment when I encountered God on the bridge—how He called me during that ORU chapel service to stand beside Dr. Cerullo and help him in the ministry.

So you can imagine the certainty I felt as I walked out of that chapel that spring morning. After such a powerful experience with God, I was convinced that as soon as I contacted the Morris Cerullo World Evangelism offices, they would immediately invite me to travel and minister with Dr. Cerullo.

Well... not exactly how it worked out.

"All the ministry positions are filled," the MCWE Personnel Manager, Glandon Broome, told me over the phone. "But we did just post a job opening for a cost accountant."

Not exactly the divine assignment I had envisioned!

Before coming to ORU, I had spent two years at the University of Notre Dame on a full academic scholarship. When I transferred, the ORU Admissions Office evaluated my credits and recommended that I pursue a Business Administration degree to make the most of what I had already completed. I chose Accounting. But from day one, I told myself—and the Lord—*I'll study accounting, but I'll never be an accountant!*

I didn't come to ORU to crunch numbers. I came to prepare to reach the world for Jesus. And now here I was, phone in hand, hearing about a job in accounting. I felt like I could relate to Job: *"The thing I greatly feared has come upon me!"*

Still, I mentioned—reluctantly—that I was just weeks away from graduating with a degree in accounting and agreed to receive the application.

Less than a week later, I was hired.

Discovering God's Blessing in Unlikely Places

During my first two years at MCWE, I served as a cost accountant—a role I never expected to enjoy, but one I grew to love. God's hand was clearly at work. He helped me uncover a little-known State of California tax law that allowed the ministry to retroactively recover tens of thousands of dollars in taxes we had paid on printing—expenses we were actually exempt from.

On weekends, my passion for evangelism found an outlet as I carried a ten-foot cross through the streets of San Diego. One day, a local newspaper picked up the story—and it just so happened that Dr. Cerullo saw it. Not long after, I received a handwritten note in the interoffice mail from Brother Cerullo himself, telling me how proud he and Theresa were of me. I was humbled and honored. Shortly after, I was invited to speak in our weekly MCWE chapel.

A few weeks later, I was called into the office of the Vice President of Accounting. He told me that Dr. Cerullo wanted me to pray about a possible move. I assumed it was a shift within the organization—but to my surprise, it was much more than that. It was an invitation to move my family to London to lead our European office and ministry outreaches.

In that moment, Proverbs 16:9 came alive to me: *"A man's heart plans his way, but the Lord directs his steps."*

I had never planned to work as an accountant, let alone lead international ministry operations. But sometimes, when we're willing to do the thing we didn't think we wanted to do, it can open the door to a season of doing the very thing we were born to do.

God gave Joseph a dream—but he was faithful in a prison that wasn't his plan, and in a palace that wasn't his plan. *"Until the time came to fulfill his dreams, the Lord tested Joseph's character"* (Psalm 105:19, NLT). Every dream has a time. Every dream has a test. And the key that moves us closer is often this: flexibility.

Embracing the Unexpected in Europe

I wound up serving as the European Director for MCWE for six years. I could have never imagined what God had in store...

It was during this time that the Iron Curtain fell, and an unprecedented door opened. Dr. Cerullo became the first evangelist invited to Moscow to conduct a crusade at the Olympic Stadium. Over three nights, more than 50,000 people attended and gave their lives to Christ. The nation was shaken to its core.

During my time in Europe, MCWE also became the first Christian organization to be granted a license to broadcast throughout the United Kingdom and Europe. Through our *Victory* television program on the European Super Channel, millions were reached with the Gospel every week.

God then spoke to Brother Cerullo about launching *Mission to London*—a series of one-week evangelistic campaigns that, for six consecutive years, packed out the 16,000-seat Earl's Court Auditorium. These gatherings sent shockwaves through the British Isles. Many of the largest and most influential churches in the U.K. today trace their roots back to those meetings.

As Eastern Europe opened, so did new invitations for Dr. Cerullo's spiritual breakthrough ministry to bless their nations. Once on a preliminary visit to Bucharest, Romania—while meeting with local pastors—I was unexpectedly given the chance to address 200,000 demonstrators gathered in University Plaza, right in the heart of the capital.

A Divine Appointment In Bucharest!

In the spring of 1990—just months after the brutal overthrow and execution of Nicolae and Elena Ceaușescu on Christmas Day 1989—I was sent to Bucharest, Romania, to do preliminary work for a major crusade that Dr. Cerullo had been invited to conduct. The nation was in turmoil. The streets still bore the weight of revolution. Romania was in the early, fragile days of rediscovering what freedom could look like—and deciding what kind of government would lead them into the future.

I was staying at the Intercontinental Hotel in downtown Bucharest. That night, April 1990, I was up late in my room, trying over and over again to get a call through back home to wish my daughter a happy birthday. Between the waiting and redialing, I spent time in prayer. As I looked out my hotel window, I could hear and see a crowd gathered in University Square, directly across from the hotel. Someone was speaking from the balcony of the university to a sea of people below.

Suddenly, I heard the voice of the Lord whisper to my heart: *"Tomorrow night, you will be speaking for Me from that balcony."*

That wasn't why I was in Romania. My purpose was to meet with local pastors, visit churches, and prepare the way for Dr. Cerullo's upcoming visit. Still, the prompting was unmistakable.

I called my translator and asked him to come an hour earlier than planned the next morning. At 8 a.m., we walked down to University Square. Though the crowd had thinned from the night before, people were still gathered, kneeling at makeshift shrines—memorials to their sons and daughters who had been killed during the uprising. Many wore campaign buttons representing the candidate they hoped would lead the new Romania. As I shared quietly with individuals, I pinned a badge on myself that simply said *Jesus*.

My translator drifted over to a nearby group being addressed by a woman. There were several hundred people gathered around her. He spoke to the student leader overseeing the group and told him I was from America and had a message to share. At first, the leader resisted: *"We don't want any American propaganda,"* he said.

But when the woman finished speaking—her message focused on the blood that had been shed for their freedom—the student leader turned to the crowd and said, *"This man is from America and wants to talk to us about Jesus. In the interest of democracy, I will let you decide if we want to hear him."*

To my amazement, the crowd responded in Romanian: *"We want to hear him."*

With a microphone now in my hand, I looked out across the square and began to speak.

"The blood that was shed in this square was not shed in vain—it was the price of freedom."

Heads nodded, and hearts connected.

Then I continued, *"Two thousand years ago, God sent His Son to this earth to shed His blood for a greater freedom—freedom from sin, from fear, from death, from separation from God. And His arms are open to you right here, right now."*

When I asked how many wanted to receive the power of that blood and take His hand, hands shot up across the crowd.
Then, something remarkable happened. The entire group knelt. Hundreds of people—right there in the square—bowed and prayed with me to receive Christ.

As they rose to their feet, they began to speak again. My translator turned to me and said, *"They're saying, 'We want to hear more.'"*

I told him we couldn't stay—we were already running behind for our pastors' meeting. But then the student leader, now with tears in his eyes, asked my translator, *"Please ask him if he will return tonight. I am the one who decides who speaks from the balcony each evening. I want Greg to come back and share with the full crowd what he shared with us this morning."*

That night, I returned. The student leader was waiting for us and took us up to a room behind the balcony. When I stepped out, I was stunned. There were at least 100,000 people—maybe closer to 200,000—packed into University Square.

As I looked over the massive crowd, I shared the same message:
"The blood shed in this square was not in vain—it purchased your freedom."
Then I declared, *"And 2,000 years ago, God sent His Son to shed His blood for your eternal freedom."*

As those words left my lips, the crowd erupted in unison—in English—chanting, *"God is with us! God is with us! God is with us!"*

It was one of the most sacred moments of my life. That night, I led one of the largest crowds I've ever seen in a prayer to receive Jesus Christ. From that moment on, the student leader declared that every night, a local Romanian pastor or evangelist would speak from the balcony to proclaim the Gospel.

And to think—it all started because I said yes to a job I never wanted. I only ended up in that square, in that moment, because

I was willing to be flexible... to serve where I was needed... to support another man's vision.

God said, *"You will accomplish more if you serve someone else."* That night in Bucharest was one more undeniable proof of the blessing of serving another man's ministry.

Flexibility Releases God's Blessing

Flexibility will always remain a powerful secret to releasing the blessing and favor of God as you serve another person's ministry. The call to serve often comes in ways we don't expect—at times and in roles we may feel unqualified for. But if we resist the urge to shrink back and instead embrace those moments, we'll find they are often the very opportunities God uses to stretch, grow, and bless us.

I'll never forget when Dr. Cerullo asked me—on just one day's notice—to be his on-air co-host for our worldwide prayer reality program *Helpline.* For the next three years, we filmed the show from CBS Studios. The program received over 1.5 million calls for prayer, and tens of thousands prayed the prayer of salvation for the first time.

Those who know me well know that I've never sought the spotlight. Being asked to co-host *Helpline,* to emcee our major events, or to lead worship has always required me to step outside my comfort zone. But each time, I chose to say yes—to be obedient, to be flexible—and each time, I watched the blessing of God flow in ways I never imagined.

"I have learned to be content in whatever circumstances I find myself." (Philippians 4:11). That kind of contentment doesn't come from ease—it comes from trusting God enough to stay flexible. Flexibility allows you to walk in peace and confidence, even when the unexpected interrupts your plans.

Secret #4: The Secret of Flexibility
Be willing to bend when God (or your mentor) redirects your path. Say yes when He calls you to step into something new. Then, watch the miracles of God flow as you follow Him into uncharted territory. Blessed are the flexible—for step by step, each step will be a miracle.

Your Call to Action: The Blessing of Flexibility

1. Where might God be inviting you to step out of your comfort zone?
Sometimes we resist change—not because we're unwilling, but because we're afraid we won't do it perfectly, or that it might expose a weakness. But the blessing often comes *after* we take the step, not before. Just as Peter discovered when he stepped out of the boat, you may find that the very thing you've been hesitant to do is where Jesus is waiting to meet you.

2. Have you mistaken discomfort for misdirection?
Some of God's greatest blessings arrive in assignments we never would have chosen for ourselves. Think back—has God ever used an unexpected moment to position you for something greater? Let those testimonies fuel your courage to say yes again.

3. Pray this prayer:
Lord, help me to trust You enough to leave my comfort zone. Make me flexible in Your hands. I don't want fear of imperfection or the risk of failure to hold me back from the miracle You've prepared. Just as Peter stepped onto the water at Your word, I choose to step out in faith, knowing You will meet me there. Use even my weakness to fulfill Your purpose through my life.

Remember, flexibility is not weakness—it's wisdom. It's the mark of a servant who trusts the Master Builder, even when the blueprint changes. Blessed are the flexible... for they will walk step by step into the miraculous!

Chapter Five

The Secret of Faithfulness

"Loyalty makes a person attractive..."
Proverbs 19:22

We live in a world that celebrates moving on—jumping from one relationship to the next, from one commitment to another. Faithfulness has often taken a backseat to self-interest. Sadly, even in the church, this pattern can be seen as believers drift from one church, ministry, or message to another—asking, "What's in it for me?" and choosing what feels good or what's most convenient—rather than staying steadfast where God has planted them. Longevity and faithfulness come with great blessing and fruitfulness.

In God's eyes, faithfulness is a treasure. Like honor, it is highly valued in heaven even if it's undervalued in our culture. The Bible says, "Loyalty makes a person attractive" (Proverbs 19:22 NLT) and asks the searching question, "Many claim to have unfailing love, but a faithful person who can find?" (Proverbs 20:6 NIV). God's Word promises, "Those who are planted in the house of the LORD shall flourish in the courts of our God" (Psalm 92:13 NKJV). Faithfulness may be rare, but it is the pathway to flourishing, lasting blessing, and God's promotion.

Faithfulness means holding firmly and devotedly to a person, cause, or calling—remaining steady in allegiance and affection; loyal and constant. Scripture makes it clear:

"Moreover, it is required in stewards that one be found faithful."
(1 Corinthians 4:2)

Faithfulness Is Rare and Precious

Over the years I have witnessed how rare true faithfulness is. Many start strong when they receive an assignment, but over time enthusiasm fades. Distractions creep in, convenience takes over, or many go looking for something "bigger and better."

Faithfulness is different. It keeps showing up. It stays steady and dependable. It does what it said it would do—consistently, even when it's costly or inconvenient. As the psalmist cried out, "Help, Lord, for no one is faithful anymore; those who are loyal have vanished from the human race" (Psalm 12:1 NIV). In a world where loyalty is rare, faithfulness shines like a priceless gem—and it never goes unnoticed by God.

The truth is, faithfulness will always be tested. "Until the time came to fulfill his dreams, the Lord tested Joseph's character" (Psalm 105:19 NLT). Every dream has a test, and every dream has a time. Joseph was faithful. Elisha was faithful. And just like in a marriage, there are moments when you have to go back to the question: *Did God bring us together?* If He did, you hold on to that calling.

For me, that moment came at Oral Roberts University, when God made it clear that He was calling me to stand by the side of Dr. Morris Cerullo and help him in the ministry. Yes, over the years, I've had other offers and opportunities, and yes—my faithfulness has been tested. But looking back now, forty years later, I can see the fruit of staying where God planted me. By His help, I've been able to serve and remain faithful to a vision that is now reaching more people—with Dr. Cerullo's voice and dream—than when he was alive.

And here's the greater truth: when we remain faithful, we reflect the very character of God Himself. The greatest trait of our God is His faithfulness to us, and when we are faithful, we reveal the image of the One who created and called us to be like Him!

The Key to Faithfulness: Knowing Your Calling

The key to faithfulness is knowing the will and calling of God. Someone once said, *"You're either called or you're crazy."* If God has called you to serve another man's ministry, or to marry your spouse, that original calling becomes the bedrock of your commitment—especially in trying times.

Above all, your faithfulness is not just to another person; it is first and foremost to the high calling of God in Christ Jesus for your life. Jesus said, *"If you have not been faithful in that which is another man's, who shall give you that which is your own?"* (Luke 16:12). That verse lays down a divine principle: faithfulness in another man's vision is God's qualification for entrusting you with your own.

I have never seen this as a license to treat my service to Dr. Cerullo as a steppingstone to my own ministry. Over the years, I've turned down opportunities that might have been seen as taking advantage of the platform he entrusted to me. Instead, I have preferred—under God—to stay single-minded, faithful one day at a time, to His call and to His servant. And in the process, I have already received more than I could ever have asked or imagined.

Here's what I know—and you can know it too: your future will take care of itself as you remain faithful to God, to His Kingdom, and to the people He has called you to serve. Jesus promised,

"Seek first the Kingdom of God and His righteousness, and all these things will be added unto you" (Matthew 6:33). God is looking for a few faithful men and women—and I believe you are one of them.

What a reward it will be to hear Him say on that great day: *"Well done, good and faithful servant! Enter into the joy of the Lord."*

Faithfulness Builds Trust

One of the greatest rewards of faithfulness is trust. When a mentor begins to recognize that they have a faithful person by their side, something changes. They begin to give that person more authority, more opportunity, and a deeper place in their confidence. The relationship moves from simply a work relationship to more of a family relationship. You become a true partner in ministry, and your input is valued in a greater way.

This was one of the great joys of my relationship with Dr. Cerullo. Over the years, as he saw that I could be counted on, he trusted me with greater responsibility. That trust was not built overnight—it grew as I consistently followed through on what I was given to do and sought to do it with excellence. It is the same principle now in serving our president, David Cerullo, as we work together to fulfill the vision of Morris Cerullo World Evangelism.

Faithfulness builds trust, and trust produces greater results. Jesus said, *"Whoever can be trusted with very little can also be trusted with much..."* (Luke 16:10). When you are faithful in the little things, both God and those you serve will entrust you with greater things.

Faithfulness Will Be Tested

There have been seasons in my years at MCWE when I felt stretched thin. The days were long, the demands were high, and at times the sacrifices seemed unnoticed. That's when I learned a vital truth: faithfulness is not proven when everything is easy—it's proven when everything is hard.

Paul exhorted Timothy, *"Endure hardship as a good soldier of Jesus Christ"* (2 Timothy 2:3). Faithfulness means you keep going when you feel like quitting. It means serving when there's no applause, staying the course when you feel overlooked, and showing up when the circumstances are far from ideal.

In those moments, God often brought me back to Colossians 3:23: *"Whatever you do, work at it with all your heart, as working for the Lord, not for human masters."* When you remember that your service is first and foremost unto God, you can remain faithful—even when others don't see, don't acknowledge, or don't understand.

The Bible gives us examples of people whose faithfulness not only stood the test of time but multiplied the impact of the work they were part of. One of those is Joshua. For decades, Joshua served as Moses' assistant—standing with him in battle, waiting with him on Mount Sinai, and remaining by his side even in seasons of challenge and uncertainty.

Joshua's role was not about seeking a platform for himself; it was about staying true to the mission God had given to Moses and making sure that mission moved forward. Because of that faithfulness, when the time came to step into the next chapter, Joshua didn't start from scratch—he carried forward the same vision, and the reach of that vision expanded to new territory. His loyalty helped ensure that what God started through Moses would continue and grow.

That's what I've experienced. Faithfulness doesn't always mean you'll step into "your own" ministry. Sometimes it means that, through your faithfulness, the ministry you've been called to will go further and touch more lives than ever before. And that is one of the greatest rewards you could ever hope for...hearing the words on that Great Day, "Well done, good and FAITHFUL servant!"

Faithfulness in Relationships

Faithfulness is not only about completing tasks—it's about cultivating and protecting relationships. Proverbs 17:17 says, *"A friend loves at all times, and a brother is born for adversity."* True faithfulness shows itself not just in easy moments but in the difficult seasons, when loyalty and constancy are tested.

One of the clearest ways to demonstrate faithfulness in relationships is by protecting and honoring those you serve. You refuse to let offense take root. You refuse to give place to gossip. Instead, you cover your leader in prayer, stand with them in challenges, and remain supportive even when others criticize.

Scripture gives us a powerful example in the life of David. Even when Saul pursued him unjustly, David refused to speak against or harm the one God had placed in leadership over Israel. He said, *"The Lord forbid that I should do such a thing to my master, the Lord's anointed"* (1 Samuel 24:6). David's choice wasn't about Saul's perfection—it was about David's own commitment to honor God by honoring the position and the person God had appointed.

Early in my service to Dr. Cerullo, I made a similar commitment—to honor him not only through my actions, but in my words and attitudes. For me, faithfulness meant guarding his reputation, choosing unity over division, and standing with him even when I might not have agreed with every decision. That kind of loyalty deepened our relationship and strengthened the ministry we were building together. It's the same spirit of faithfulness I seek to walk in today as I serve our president, David Cerullo, in carrying forward the vision of Morris Cerullo World Evangelism.

Faithfulness Leads to Promotion And Greater Fruitfulness

Every advancement I've experienced in ministry has been the direct result of faithfulness—but the greatest reward hasn't been a title or position. I have seen greater fruitfulness in my role, greater impact in the work God has entrusted to me, and blessing overflowing into my family, my relationships, and my personal life. Faithfulness doesn't just change where you serve—it changes how you serve and the results that follow.

In the parable of the talents, Jesus commended the servant who invested what he was given wisely: *"Well done, good and faithful servant! You have been faithful with a few things; I will put you in charge of many things"* (Matthew 25:21). God's promotion is not something we campaign for—it is the natural byproduct of being faithful where He has planted us.

John Maxwell once said, *"Success is adding value to yourself. Significance is adding value to someone else."* Faithfulness, at its core, will take you beyond success into significance. It will allow your life to be used by God to add lasting value to the people and vision you serve. And that, to me, is the real blessing of faithfulness.

Brother Cerullo often reminded me, *"Greg, if God can trust you, He will bless you."* I have seen that proven true again and again. Scripture promises, *"A faithful man will abound with blessings..."* (Proverbs 28:20). And the greatest blessing of all is knowing that the value you've added, through faithfulness, will bear fruit that remains for eternity.

The Secret of Faithfulness

To recap: Faithfulness isn't glamorous, but it is powerful. It will set you apart in a world that prizes convenience over commitment. When you choose to be faithful—to God, to your calling, and to the people He has entrusted you to serve—you unlock blessings, influence, and opportunities that only God can open.

Secret #5: The Secret of Faithfulness — Be steady. Be loyal. Be consistent. Faithfulness will unlock the blessing of God and position you for greater fruitfulness in life and ministry.

Chapter Takeaways:
- Faithfulness is not measured in moments but in seasons.

- The real blessing of faithfulness is greater fruitfulness and significance, not just personal promotion.

- When you remain faithful, you reflect the very character of God, whose greatest attribute is His faithfulness to us.

- Faithfulness builds trust, and trust opens the door to greater influence and partnership.

- Every test of faithfulness is an opportunity to show God—and others—that you can be trusted with more.

Your Call to Action:

1. Identify where God is calling you to stand firm.
Is there an assignment, relationship, or area of service where you've been tempted to "move on" for the sake of comfort, convenience, or something that looks "bigger and better"? Ask the Holy Spirit to confirm where He has planted you and renew your commitment to be faithful there.

2. Guard the relationships God has entrusted to you.
Faithfulness isn't just about doing the work—it's about protecting and honoring the people you serve. Pray for them, refuse to let offense take root, and cover them in both your words and your actions.

3. Serve as unto the Lord.
Colossians 3:23 reminds us, *"Whatever you do, work at it with all your heart, as working for the Lord, not for human masters."* When you remember that your service is to God first, you can remain faithful even when others don't see or acknowledge it.

Let's pray this prayer:
Lord, help me to be faithful in the place where You have planted me. Keep my heart steady, my spirit loyal, and my service consistent—whether I am seen or unseen. May my life reflect Your faithfulness, and may the fruit of my faithfulness bring glory to You and advance Your Kingdom, Amen!

Chapter Six

The Secret Of Being Proactive

Anticipate the need. Protect the vision. Advance the mission.

One of the greatest privileges—and most rewarding opportunities—you can experience in serving another man's ministry is found in **the secret of being a proactive servant**.

A proactive person is "one who creates or controls a situation by causing something to happen rather than simply responding to it after it happens." In other words, they don't just wait for instructions—they anticipate needs, take initiative, and find ways to add value before being asked.

A fruitful, effective disciple is much more than an order taker. Over time, as you prove yourself faithful, a foundation of trust is built. That trust becomes the key ingredient that allows you to move from simply carrying out tasks to becoming a true partner in the vision—someone who is not just serving in the ministry, but actively helping to shape and advance it.

The Moscow 1989 Story

I will never forget Moscow, 1989.

For fourteen consecutive years, from the platform of London's world-renowned Royal Albert Hall, Dr. Cerullo boldly prophesied that Russia's Iron Curtain would come down and the Soviet Union would open in an unprecedented way to the preaching of the Gospel.

In the late 1980s, that prophecy began to unfold. A wave of democratization—known as *Perestroika*—was sweeping across the Soviet Union under General Secretary Mikhail Gorbachev, and long-closed doors were beginning to creak open.

One afternoon in the fall of 1989, the beep of the fax machine in our European office signaled an incoming message. I picked it up to find an extraordinary invitation from the President of the Russian Pentecostal Union, Rev. Bilas Roman. He was asking Brother Cerullo to come to Moscow as the first Christian leader in the *Perestroika* era to conduct an open, public crusade.

I immediately shared the invitation with Brother Cerullo and booked a flight to Moscow to meet with Rev. Bilas and the leaders of the Pentecostal Union. Many of these pastors had endured imprisonment and persecution for their faith, yet they radiated a deep hunger for a genuine move of God that would touch their nation with the power of the Holy Spirit. As I sat across from them, I could see in their eyes both the pain of what they had suffered and the anticipation of what might now be possible.

Together, we prayed and began planning a great one-night crusade at the historic 7,000-seat Ismailova Sports Hall on the outskirts of Moscow. This was no small undertaking—Russia was just emerging from decades of communism. Printing was scarce, and there were no commercial advertising channels available. Eventually, we managed to design and print 20,000 crusade flyers at a small Alpha Graphics shop in Moscow. I left the leaders with the flyers, a mobilization plan, and a prayer strategy to spread the word, confident that the groundwork had been laid.

Months later, I returned to Moscow—only to discover that the flyers had not been distributed. Fear and uncertainty had held the leaders back. When I asked how people would know about the crusade, they replied, "We have been praying... and we have arranged for Dr. Cerullo to be interviewed on the Moscow News the night before the meeting."

God Moves Mightily on Live TV

When Dr. Cerullo arrived in Moscow for the crusade, I followed my normal practice of not burdening him with any challenges unless they were truly critical. So, I didn't mention that none of the flyers had been distributed or that our situation was far from ideal. Instead, I simply shared the good news that he had been invited to be interviewed that evening on the Moscow News, and together we headed to the studio.

What was scheduled as a one- or two-minute segment that evening turned into nearly 30 minutes as the presence of God filled the studio. The host, visibly moved, asked Dr. Cerullo to pray for the viewers to receive Christ. Then, she invited him to pray for physical healing. As he prayed, the phones at the station lit up with callers testifying of salvation and miraculous healings.

That night, when our interpreter returned home, his elderly atheist neighbor was waiting for him. She told him that as she watched the program, she felt a deep heat in her back and was instantly healed of a debilitating spinal condition she had suffered with for years. Right there on her porch, she prayed with him to receive Jesus as her Savior.

God was shaking a nation—before we had even stepped onto the crusade platform.

A Crowd That Couldn't Be Contained

The next afternoon, the anticipation from the night before had reached a fever pitch. Even after the doors to the Ismailova Auditorium were opened three hours early and every one of its 7,000 seats was filled, the crowds kept coming. Before long, they were standing ten-deep around the entire arena, straining for any chance to get inside.

What began as eager expectancy was quickly turning into frustration. People pressed against the entrances. Windows were breaking. The police insisted that the church leaders persuade Dr. Cerullo to cancel the meeting so they could disperse the crowd before things got out of hand.

The top leaders approached me, visibly shaken, and asked to speak with Dr. Cerullo to request that he postpone the meeting. But my role was clear: it was never to disturb him with negative reports before a service, but to find solutions so he could remain undistracted and focused in his customary time of prayer, fasting, and preparation.

This was a moment to be proactive. Standing there with the Russian leaders looking to me for an answer, I quietly prayed for God's wisdom. Then an idea came:

"What if," I said, "we take the many boxes containing the 5,000 brand-new Bibles we had planned to give to new converts inside, and instead bring them out to the people who can't get in—along with the promise that Dr. Cerullo will return to Moscow soon for a larger stadium crusade?"

They agreed immediately. Within minutes, the police were carrying boxes of Bibles to the crowd outside. The people received them as if they had just been handed treasure. Smiles replaced frustration, peace was restored, and the assurance of a return visit gave everyone something to look forward to.

That day, what could have become a serious crisis turned into an opportunity for the Gospel. And it happened because, in a moment of challenge, we stayed focused on the mission and found a way to bless the very people who couldn't get inside. Moments like this remind us that being a proactive servant means more than solving problems—it's about protecting the vision, honoring the leader you serve, and finding creative ways to keep the door open for God to touch people's lives.

The Night The Power Of God Fell In Moscow!

That night was one of the most glorious services I have ever been a part of—but it didn't start that way.

When Dr. Morris and Theresa Cerullo arrived at the Ismailova Auditorium, the crowds outside made it impossible for them to enter through any secure entrance. We had arranged for pastors to meet them and bring them inside, but as soon as the people recognized Dr. Cerullo from his television interview the night before, a surge swept toward him. It was almost like the scene of the woman with the issue of blood pressing through the crowd to touch the hem of Jesus' garment—people reaching, desperate for a touch.

Inside, 7,000 people filled every seat, and easily 95 percent of them were not believers. The atmosphere was flat—there was no sense of the presence of God. The singing was slow and heavy, almost like a funeral dirge. I have never looked forward more to handing a meeting over to Dr. Cerullo. He was scheduled to be on the platform at 7:30, but 7:30 came and went... 7:40... still no sign. At 7:50—twenty minutes late, which was unlike him—Morris and

Theresa finally stepped onto the platform, looking as though they had just been through a storm. Only later did I learn the challenges they had faced getting inside.

When I took the microphone that night and said, "Would you join me in welcoming God's servant, Dr. Morris Cerullo..." it was one of the greatest feelings of relief I can remember! But what happened next was beyond anything I could have imagined.

Dr. Cerullo didn't raise his voice or work the crowd into emotion. Instead, he simply began to tell the Gospel story from the book of Genesis—how God never intended for sin, sickness, or death to enter the world; how, because of Adam's sin, the curse came and brought sin, sickness, and death; and how God sent His Son, Jesus Christ, to take the curse upon Himself and break its power through the sacrifice of His life.

He spoke calmly, under the anointing of the Holy Spirit, and when he finished, he didn't call people forward—he simply invited them to talk to God right where they were. That's when it happened. Demons began to scream out of people. The power and presence of God swept through the room. Miracles began to break out across the auditorium.

Literally everyone in the building prayed the prayer of salvation, and the atmosphere was transformed. We hadn't even had time to train altar workers—earlier in the afternoon the crowds had been so large that we simply opened the doors to let people in. Yet God Himself moved among the people. Blind eyes opened. The lame began to walk.

One woman I will never forget was the assistant to the president of the Baptist Union in Moscow. She had been confined to a wheelchair for years, and her office had even built a special ramp so she could come to work. That night, the Lord touched her, and she rose from her wheelchair completely healed.

CNN was in the building that night, doing a story on religious freedom in the era of *Perestroika*. They captured not just the event, but the undeniable evidence that God was moving in Russia in a new way.

That night marked the beginning of a great revival. Less than six months later, we returned to Moscow—this time to the 15,000-seat Olympic Stadium—for three consecutive capacity nights, with nearly 50,000 precious Russians in total giving their lives to Christ.

"I have planted, Apollos watered, but God gave the increase. So then neither is he that planteth anything, neither he that watereth, but God that giveth the increase" (1 Corinthians 3:6–7).

It all began with a challenge, a prayer for wisdom, and a determination to protect and serve the man of God so he could focus on the message God had given him. The rest was God's doing—and the glory was all His.

What Proactivity Produces

As the mentor–mentee relationship grows over time, you begin to know the heart of the man or woman you are serving and understand what they would expect in certain situations. This insight makes you far more valuable as a servant. Instead of simply waiting for instructions, you can anticipate needs and become a creative contributor to the overall vision and purpose of your leader and their ministry.

While Dr. Cerullo was the unquestioned visionary and strong spiritual leader of MCWE, one of his great strengths as a mentor was his humility and his expectation that key team members operate with both authority and spiritual freedom to bring creative ideas and input to the table—on any and every aspect of the ministry.

Some of the most successful outreaches in MCWE history were birthed out of this synergy between Dr. Cerullo and our team.

Our shared passion and creativity fueled "God ideas" that became reality because we had the trust to bring them forward—and the commitment to see them through. A word to the wise: don't bring an idea to your leader unless you are ready to take responsibility for helping make it happen!

So, are you ready to take your next step in serving another person's ministry? If you see a need in your church or ministry that is not being filled, maybe God is calling you to be the one to fill it—without waiting to be asked and without expecting someone else to do it. That is the secret of a proactive servant, and it will open the door for God to use you in ways you never imagined.

How to Practice Proactive Servanthood

- **Anticipate needs.** Ask, "What will be needed two steps from now?" Prepare before you're asked.

- **Bring solutions.** When you raise a problem, propose a pathway forward.

- **Protect focus.** Shield your leader from avoidable noise before a major assignment.

- **Own the outcome.** Treat the ministry's success as your personal responsibility.

- **Stay aligned.** Keep your initiative in step with the leader's heart and the ministry's mission.

Your Call to Action: The Secret of Being a Proactive Servant

1. Learn the heart of the one you serve.
Ask God to help you understand not only your leader's words, but their values, vision, and priorities. The better you know their heart, the more effectively you can anticipate needs and take initiative.

2. Turn your observations into action.
If you see a need, don't just point it out—prayerfully step in to meet it. Proactive servants look for ways to add value without waiting to be asked.

3. Own the ideas God gives you.
Don't bring a suggestion to the table unless you're willing to help carry it out. Initiative paired with responsibility builds trust and multiplies your influence.

Pray this prayer:
Lord, make me a proactive servant in Your Kingdom. Help me to know the heart of those You have called me to serve, to see needs through Your eyes, and to step in with faith, humility, and excellence. May my actions advance the vision You have entrusted to my leaders, and may I serve in such a way that brings You glory.

Secret #6: The Secret of Being Proactive — Don't just show up. *Step up.* Think ahead. Carry the burden. Bring solutions. When you serve this way, you position yourself for favor, authority and multiplication.

Chapter Seven

Receiving the Mantle of Your Mentor

Where Is The Lord God of Morris Cerullo?

"He also took up the mantle of Elijah that had fallen from him, and went back and stood by the bank of the Jordan. Then he took the mantle of Elijah that had fallen from him, and struck the water, and said, 'Where is the Lord God of Elijah?' And when he also had struck the water, it was divided this way and that; and Elisha crossed over." (2 Kings 2:13–14)

The Key To Receiving The Mantle Of Your Mentor

Throughout the more than three decades I served Dr. Morris Cerullo, I came to realize that one of the driving forces of his life was not just preaching the Gospel, but imparting what God had placed in him into the lives of others. This was not a side mission—it was the heartbeat of his ministry. On some level this should be a key element of every mentor and ministry you will serve.

He often recounted a defining moment in 1962 when the Lord gave him the experience that would shape everything he did from that day forward. God asked him, *"Son, what do you want out of this life?"* And Morris replied, *"God, give me the ability to give to somebody else what You've given to me."* In that moment, God spoke to him and said, *"Son, build Me an army."*

From that day on, his calling was no longer only to win souls, but to multiply himself—to raise up others who could walk in the same grace, anointing and authority God had given him. Like Jesus and the twelve, Morris' ministry became a ministry of multiplication and impartation.

One of the great honors of serving his ministry was knowing that while the work was hard, it was also deeply rewarding. I knew he wasn't just trying to get something from me—he was trying to get something to me. Many times, he would say, *"Greg, what God has placed in me must get into you."* And that wasn't just a statement for the future when he would no longer be on the earth—it was something I experienced continually during our 30-plus years together.

The key to receiving the mantle of your mentor is that it's not automatic. It doesn't "just happen" because you're close to them or because you admire them. Elijah told Elisha, *"If you see me when I am taken from you, it shall be so for you"* (2 Kings 2:10). Elijah even tried to shake Elisha off three different times, but Elisha refused to leave his side. His persistence proved the depth of his heart connection. He honored his mentor, obeyed his instructions, and stayed faithful until the end. **Impartation flowed through connection.**

It is the same today. Receiving from your mentor requires that you embrace the same six secrets we've covered in this book: honor, obedience, flexibility, faithfulness, being proactive, and staying relationally connected.

This is one of the greatest joys and benefits of serving another person's ministry—the blessing that comes not just by association, but by impartation. You see firsthand how your mentor responds to challenges, makes decisions, and relies on God's wisdom. Often, those moments become a storehouse of empowerment and lessons you will draw from when you face similar situations in the future.

Like Elisha, you position yourself to carry forward not only the mantle, but the spirit and the wisdom of the one you serve—so that the work of God does not end with them, but continues and multiplies through you.

The Day Dr. Cerullo Went Home

On July 10, 2020, at approximately 2:00 a.m., I received the heart wrenching news that Morris Cerullo had breathed his last breath on earth and his first breath in the presence of the Lord. Jeri and I stayed up the rest of the morning reflecting on his life and legacy. I wrote the tribute that I shared in the Prologue. By 6:00 a.m., we drove to the Legacy International Center.

We parked in the employee parking lot, and without even thinking, I threw myself down onto the asphalt. I cried out to God with everything in me, *"Lord, give me the ability. Give me the anointing. Help me to continue to honor and extend the legacy that Dr. Morris and Teresa Cerullo established over seven decades of reaching the nations of the world."*

Anointings Never Leave the Earth

Pastor Rod Parsley once made a statement that has stayed with me: *"Anointings never leave the earth. They either lie dormant, or, if you pick them up, they intensify."*

It has now been over five years since Dr. Cerullo went home to be with the Lord, and I can truly say that his anointing has not left us—it has intensified.

I do not call myself the successor of Dr. Cerullo. God spoke to him to raise up an **army** of successors. But I did have the great privilege of standing by his side, learning from him, and receiving his impartation. Now I get to carry forward the vision he lived and died for.

People often ask me, *"Greg, now that Dr. Cerullo is gone, what are you doing?"* My answer is simple: **"I'm doing the same thing I was doing when he was alive. I am serving the vision of my mentor, Dr. Morris Cerullo."**

Serving the Vision and Our President

Today, I also have the honor of serving our president, David Cerullo—Morris and Theresa Cerullo's oldest son and the president of Morris Cerullo World Evangelism. My role is different now, but the calling is the same: to steward the mantle that was placed upon us and to carry the vision forward.

It is one of my greatest privileges to serve David, serve our partners, and serve the vision that God gave to Dr. Cerullo. One of the great blessings—and challenges—of this season is leaning even more fully on the Lord. I often ask myself: *What would Dr. Cerullo do in this situation?*

I can say without hesitation that if I had not received from Dr. Cerullo the grace, wisdom, and anointing that I did, I would not be able to serve David Cerullo, our partners, and this ministry in the way that God has enabled us to in this new legacy season.

"And the things you have heard me say in the presence of many witnesses entrust to reliable people who will also be qualified to teach others." (2 Timothy 2:2)

A Legacy That Is Still Bearing Fruit

As I write this edition of the book, it is such a joy to report that Dr. Cerullo's life and ministry continue to produce fruit that remains. His voice and vision are touching more lives now than ever before:

- **Online School of Ministry:** Dr. Cerullo's teaching and voice is now training more leaders worldwide than at any time in history. Hundreds of thousands of students from every nation are enrolling, learning, and equipping themselves to fulfill the Great Commission through the Morris Cerullo God's Victorious Army Online School of Ministry. (www.mcwe.com/gvasom)

- **Morris Cerullo Digital Salvation Outreach:** Every single minute, at least one person is telling us, *"This is my name, this is my email address. I have received the miracle of salvation through the Morris Cerullo Digital Salvation Outreach."* This outreach features a powerful salvation prayer that Dr. Cerullo prayed years ago at Earl's Court in London and is now seeing more souls come to Christ than when he was alive!

- **The Legacy International Center:** What began as a dream in Dr. Cerullo's heart is now a thriving hub of ministry, hospitality, and community outreach. The Legacy Center is impacting lives daily and standing as a living monument to the power of vision and faith.

- **Global Leaders Continuing the Work:** Millions of leaders worldwide who were personally trained and impacted through Dr. Cerullo's life and ministry are continuing to expand and extend the ministry's impact, multiplying the anointing they received into countless lives and ministries across the globe.

- **Enlarging My Impact:** God has also been working in me personally. Tommy Barnett once gave me one of the greatest compliments I have ever received when he called me *"America's number one, number two man."* He was saying that I have embraced the call of standing alongside another man's vision and being excellent at serving it. In this season, I am using the grace and impartation I received through serving Dr. Cerullo to faithfully serve our president, David Cerullo, the partners of this ministry, and the vision God entrusted to Dr. Cerullo. God has taken me out of my comfort zone—I am preaching more, teaching more, encouraging more, and representing Dr. Cerullo in places where now he is not here. In every situation, God has shown Himself strong on our behalf, and we are moving forward with confidence and courage as a result of the faithful impartation that I have received from the Lord and through my mentor, Dr. Morris Cerullo.

- "You did not choose Me, but I chose you and appointed you so that you might go and bear fruit—fruit that will last." (John 15:16)

How Do You Receive the Mantle of Your Mentor?

Receiving the mantle of your mentor is not automatic. It requires relationship, honor, and hunger.

- **Relationship:** Elisha didn't just observe Elijah from a distance—he walked closely with him. Impartation flows through connection.

- **Honor:** Elisha called Elijah "my father." He respected the grace on his life and served him wholeheartedly.

- **Obedience and Flexibility:** He obeyed without hesitation and adjusted his life to follow Elijah wherever God led.

- **Faithfulness:** He refused to abandon his mentor even when Elijah told him to stay behind.

- **Proactive Service:** He looked for ways to help and prepare for the future, not just react to what was happening in the moment.

- **Hunger:** Elisha refused to settle for less than a double portion. He stayed close until the very end.

If you want to receive the mantle of your mentor, position yourself as Elisha did. Serve faithfully. Stay hungry. Keep your heart pure.

Anointings Are for Every Area of Service

Before we close, let me encourage you with this: anointings and mantles are not just given to preach. God desires to place and increase His anointing in your life to serve in many different areas. In Scripture, over 3,000 individuals are named as men and women who served Him in diverse capacities—prophets, kings, armor bearers, artisans, intercessors, administrators, musicians, financiers, and more. God is not only anointing "number ones," but He is anointing number twos, threes, and fours, empowering people to serve in ways that often go unnoticed by man but are deeply valued by Him. Whether you are called to lead from the front or to serve faithfully behind the scenes, there is a mantle for you.

For some, receiving the mantle of your mentor and the blessing of serving their ministry will eventually lead to a season of promotion, where God gives you what Jesus called *"your own"*: *"If you have not been faithful in what is another man's, who will give you what is your own?"* (Luke 16:12). For others—and for me personally—the call to serve as a number two is the calling I will carry into eternity. The blessing I have received has not been in a change of title or position, but in the increased favor, the greater results, the multiplied impact, opportunities to preach, and the joy of watching the work continue to grow and expand. I have seen God's blessing overflow into my family, my physical health, my personal life, my relationships, my finances, my effectiveness at MCWE, and my ability to help multiply the kingdom of God.

Yes, for some there will be an Elijah and Elisha, a Moses and Joshua. But for many others, God's promotion and reward will not be measured only by a new role—it will be measured in your effectiveness, your fruitfulness, and the eternal results you get to be part of. Truly, the words the Lord spoke to me on that bridge at Oral Roberts University have come to pass again and again: by serving another man's ministry, I am accomplishing more for the kingdom than if I were serving myself and my prayer is that will be your experience as well.

Closing Prayer and Declaration

Allow me to pray with you as we close:

Father, I lift my friend to You today. I thank You for the calling You have placed on their life and for the mantle You are preparing them to receive. Lord, I ask You to reward them as they diligently seek to serve You and Your kingdom. Release a fresh anointing of Your power, Your wisdom, and Your love into their life and ministry today, in Jesus' name.

Father, I declare that as they walk in the **secret of honor**, You will raise them up. As they walk in **obedience**, they will experience Your blessing. As they remain **flexible**, they will see doors open that no man can shut. As they live out the **secret of faithfulness**, You will entrust them with more. As they choose to be **proactive**, they will be ready for every opportunity You place before them. And as they position themselves to receive the **mantle of their mentor**, they will walk in an increase of Your anointing and favor.

And now, Lord, I declare by faith that **their promotion is in motion** as they continue to honor You and honor those You have called them to serve. Thank You that the blessing of serving another man's ministry will overflow in their life, their family, and their future. We ask this and receive it with joy, in Jesus' mighty name. Amen.

About The Author

Greg Mauro has devoted nearly four decades to serving as the Vice President of Ministries for world-renowned evangelist Dr. Morris Cerullo through Morris Cerullo World Evangelism. While a student at Oral Roberts University, Greg experienced a dramatic encounter with God in 1987 that forever changed his life. In that moment, the Lord sovereignly called him to serve the ministry of Dr. Cerullo—a divine connection that would shape his destiny and become the platform for a lifetime of ministry.

Since that time Greg has faithfully carried the mantle of *serving another man's ministry*. He has traveled the world alongside Dr. Cerullo, serving as crusade director, television co-host, writer, media strategist, conference emcee, and trusted associate minister. He played a key role in historic evangelistic outreaches such as the **Mission to London crusades** at Earl's Court Arena, drawing over 17,000 nightly, the **Mission to Moscow** at the 15,000-seat Olympic Stadium, and the global **Helpline Television broadcast**, which brought salvation, healing, and prayer to millions worldwide.

Today, Greg continues in that same calling, serving under the leadership of **David Cerullo**, to help steward and expand the vision to *take the Gospel to the nations and build God an army* at the 18-acre Morris Cerullo Legacy International Center campus in San Diego, California.

As an **author and speaker**, Greg's ministry is marked by two core life messages:

- First, the profound truth that there is a **supernatural blessing in serving another man's ministry**. His life stands as a living testimony to this principle, and he continues to equip and encourage leaders and believers worldwide to embrace this pathway to legacy and promotion.

- Second, the life-changing message of *Your Promotion Is in Motion*: that **God sees something greater in you, and something greater for you, than you see for yourself**. Through this message, Greg calls believers to rise from the sidelines to success, and from success to significance—discovering that every believer is a full-time minister of the Gospel.

Greg is joyfully married to his wife, **Jeri**, and together they are blessed with **eight children** and a growing legacy of **thirteen grandchildren**. His family is a living testimony of God's faithfulness and blessing through a life of obedience and service.

If you would like to invite Greg to minister at your church, conference, or special event, you may contact him at **gregmauro1159@gmail.com**.
You can also enjoy more of his writings and ministry insights at **www.gregmauro.com**.

Photo Gallery

Moscow Red Square 1990 With Morris and Theresa Cerullo

It has been the honor of my life to have stood by the side of Dr. Cerullo for over three decades!

Cohosting Morris Cerullo Helpline From CBS Studios with Dr. Cerullo. My beautiful wife Jeri, who is now the Director of the MCWE Volunteer In Home Prayer Ministry is pictured over my left shoulder.

1990 Madrid, Spain Morris Cerullo Crusade. The night that hail stones fell inside an enclosed bull ring!

PHOTO GALLERY 61

Night after night, 16,000 people packed the world-famous Earl's Court Arena for an entire week during the Morris Cerullo Mission to London crusades—an outreach we pioneered together in the 1990s that shook Britain for six unforgettable years!

Honored to lead the salvation prayer and pray for those needing healing in Morris Cerullo's final Los Angeles Crusade.

Blessed to have Morris and Theresa join Jeri and I and our family for our daughter Christina's wedding in 2017.

One of the greatest blessings of serving Dr. Cerullo's ministry is how God has blessed our family. Morris and Theresa prayed Jeri into my life. We married in 1999 and brought eight children together — pictured here (including grandchildren) in 2023.

www.ingramcontent.com/pod-product-compliance
Lightning Source LLC
Chambersburg PA
CBHW050043080526
44586CB00014B/1438